Books by Jean Valentine

Dream Barker
Pilgrims
Ordinary Things
The Messenger

The Messenger

Farrar · Straus · Giroux / New York

The Messenger / Jean Valentine

First printing, 1979
Printed in the United States of America
Published simultaneously in Canada by
McGraw-Hill Ryerson Ltd., Toronto
Designed by Cynthia Krupat
Library of Congress Cataloging in Publication Data
Valentine, Jean. / The messenger.
Poems. / I. Title.
PS3572.A39M4 / 811'.5'4 / 79–1373

for James Shea

Acknowledgments

Some of the poems in this collection first appeared—at times in different versions—in *The American Poetry Review*; *The Blacksmith Anthology*, edited by Gail Mazur; *Field*; *Green House*; *Harvard Magazine*; *Ironwood*; *The Nation*; *The New Yorker* (*Beka*, 14; *The Messenger*); *Pequod*; *Pocket Pal*; *Transatlantic Review*; *Vanderbilt Review*.

Seven of the poems in the first part were printed as a chapbook, *Turn*, edited by Bruce Weigl, designed by Jean Kondo Weigl, Pocket Pal Press, Oberlin, Ohio, 1977.

I want to thank the John Simon Guggenheim Memorial Foundation for the grant which gave me the freedom to finish this book. And—again—my thanks to Yaddo, and to The MacDowell Colony, for their space and quiet.

The poem by Huub Oosterhuis was translated with Judith Herzberg.
The poem by Osip Mandelstam was translated with Anne Frydman.

J. V.

Contents

The Messenger

Two Translations

Solitudes

The Messenger

My name comes to me like an angel.

—Tomas Tranströmer

Susan's Photograph

for S.T.

I am the razor that has been put away, also
the wrist in the photograph,
and— lately— also the photographer,
the friend, the taxi, the hospital room,
the three other women, their visitors, the flowers,
and the nurse.

At the end of that summer
I started going to paramedical school
at night. Days I still talk to my students
about all the dead
overexcitable poets; all their friends;
and the living; and show the old newsreels
where they keep leaving each other, old
people, children, soldiers; and the parades:
the general, the waving people, the black horses, the black
limousines, the mules, the tall gray puppets.

But this photograph here:
a woman in a country room, in western Massachusetts,
in peace, so sad and grained:

> now I see you look up, outside the
> frame—

this room here, friends, a table, a book or two,
paper, I see you have all you need,
—*even in prison you would have your childhood*—

it is enough, now,
anywhere, with
everyone you love there to talk to.

Outside the Frame

It is enough, now, anywhere,
with everyone you love there to talk to.

And to listen.
Slowly we can tell each other some things about our lives:
runs, rests, brief resolutions; falls, and lulls;
hard, joyful runs, in certainty; dull, sweet
durances, human silences;
                    look back in at the children,
the regular, neutral flicker of their blood; pale, solemn,
long-legged animal-gods in their sleep,
growing into their lives, in their sleep.

—1973

Beka, 14

Squat, slant-eyed, speaking in phrase-book phrases, the messenger
says he is your brother, and settles down on his heels
to wait, muffled in flat, supple skin, rope over his shoulder. You
wait, play, turn, forget. Years,

years. The messenger is both like the penguin
who sits on the nest of pebbles, and the one
who brings home pebbles to the nest's edge in his beak,
one at a time, and also like the one
who is lying there, warm, who is going to break out soon:

becoming yourself: the messenger is growing
strong, tough feet for land,
and strong wings for the water, and long
butter-yellow feather eyebrows, for looks. And will speak,
calmly, words you already know: "thread," "island,"

"must": now, slowly, just while you lie on your cot there, half-
dozing, not reading, watching the trees,
a summer, and a summer; writing long pages, tearing them up;

lying there under the close August window, while at your back
the water-lit, dotted lines of home start coloring in.

Dufy Postcard

for S., at 50

The postcard taped on your white kitchen wall has roses, in a white
bowl, on the blue and green shadowed table; the table is brown,
yellow. Down the wallpaper's field of pink roses, a violet shadow
turns brown, moves across the floor: now the lines go off the card,
the lines of the walls, one curved foot of the round table, the
oblong shadow; the floor ends mid-air, here:

> You sitting at your table
> looking at the postcard. Green
> day lights the windows; everyone
> still asleep. Taut lines.

> Day, with its hours, and buildings;
> people start, around you. You wait
> a minute more in the white room—
> white tent against the snowed-over path, the wind,
> familiar voice— *one life*—

> Every day you move farther outside
> the outlines, kinder, more dangerous.
> Where will you be going.
> Who will the others be.

The Field

"There is a strange power in bog water which prevents decay. Bodies have been found which must have lain in bogs for more than a thousand years . . ."—A Danish Almanack of 1837.
—P. V. Glob, The Bog People

A sculpture in a bare white gallery:
Pike jaws arch, in a shining transparent space
without locality: levels of peat, sand, air.
Bones. Teeth.
Fine, thin white jaws: the willingness to do harm— Odysseus
       leaving—

At forty we have always been parents; we hold each other's sex
in a new tenderness . . . As we were; hardly breathing
over the pulse in the infant's lucent temple—

Our breath comes shorter,
our lives have been a minute, a feather, our sex is chaff . . .

Sleep: the room
breaks up into blue and red
film, long muscles crossing bones, raw pelvis pulled
to birth: Incised on stone, bronze, silver
Eyes, belly, mouth   Circle on circle—

Look, by morning noises, in this city island flickering with gold
        flame,
These photographs.
The Tollund man. The Windeby girl. The goddess
Nerthus.

In the middle of a light wood   of tall forked trees stripped white
at the edge of a bog, in Denmark,
we walk   slowly out to the field   walk slowly by
the hacked-out cots
of silk
bog children.

Living Together

Dawn, streaks of rose-brown, dry—
A car starts up. A needle veers,
an hour, a summer . . . Day
settles back, on the last
century, our trying, our Biblical
conviviality.

This should, should not, happen, these
two people met, or not then, not now;
or now.

Out in the white Judaic light
you move like figures in a lesson;

You open your life like a book.
Still I hear your story
like a parable, where every word is simple,
but how does this one
go with the one before, the next . . .

Here Now

The sky is the same changing
colors as the farthest snow.
The tall pines float
like candles with the current,
next to the stream
clear with brown leaves.

> A pitched ceiling,
> two cots; apple petals;
> the thin smell of woodsmoke,
> wood, turpentine . . .
> *My sister*, I, who
> we were then—

> Downstairs, the grown world
> bent to its books; low flames, low
> voices. Sleeplessness . . .

> Our wooden room
> —The white cloth
> on the table between us

Forty years, a breath . . . our tall daughters circle like birds, in our
light houses, bump into things
Their high words, leaving out their lives

Quiet-minded, a lightness, this morning; the piece of sea glass next
to the window, almost amber, curved like a thumb, a petal

The sky is the same changing
blue, and green, as the burning snow.
So much must be asleep
under this white quiet, sleep,
sleep, low voices, dust hair,
under the eyes
the impossible
compass fingers
of the god.

The Forgiveness Dream:
Man from the Warsaw Ghetto

for J.E.S.

He looked about six or seven, only much too thin.
It seemed right he would be there, but everything,
every lineation, was slow . . . He was speaking in Polish,
I couldn't answer him.
He pointed at the window, the trees, or the snow,
or our silver auditorium.

I said to him in English, "I've lived the whole time
here, in peace. A private life."   "In shame,"
I said. He nodded. He was old now, kind,
my age, or my mother's age: He nodded,
and wrote in my notebook— "Let it be good."

He frowned, and stopped,
as if he'd forgotten something,
and wrote again,
"Let it."

I walk, and stop, and walk—
touch the birch bark   shining, powdery, cold:
taste the snow, hot on my tongue—
pure cold, licked from the salt of my hand:

———

This quiet, these still unvisitable stars
move with choices.
Our kin are here.
Were here.

Turn

for F. and P.L.

This is the new apartment   new
painted livingroom
its table, its bed, its chair.
It is floating, and the earth's bright rim
is floating through an indifferent blank, without
color, without consolation—

> The pregnant woman with a child at home
> rests, has a cup of tea, closes her eyes . . .
> I want to walk in the winter field again . . .
> Was peacefulness
> ever what we were after?
> She thinks of the child, who wants the tea, who wants
> her eyes, her mouth, her hands,
> who pulls her out to the field
> to the thick of things
> away from the thick of things.

A woman stands   at the new window.
Torso: a bronze Matisse back:
in the Museum garden. Its children playing, still,
inside its hollow part.
Its strength thickens, simplifies.
Grows quieter.

15

The first day's quiet. The second; the second
year. I'm taking up my life. If you were here
who I am honest with
I'd have to think a long time
to say the simplest thing:
nothing like anything I know.

Prayer in Fever

The hospital shuts down to its half-night.

I stand back,
talk in words from some book:
The wall could be the floor.
Everything you look at
is changed by your looking at it

This packed dirt square, these wires . . . somewhere someone must
run for it, black hair, red mouth, burn
strips of fish on a green edge of the Hudson,
under a cloud of stars, under bridge lights, they must hunch down,
talk to each other, touch each other, the way this thin bright snow
masses, this blind oval pulling

gold   across the ceiling
floating out
off the fold-
back of space

The day does rise. The turning gaze of the river:
So many eyes. So calm.

The gray green curve of earth still
waiting   with us
holding us
huge curved mosaic hands

your hand
—how would you bide so long?

Working

in memory of Robert Lowell
1917–1977

Under the high rooms,
under the trains, the talk,
you kept digging down

from life to life
to come across earth's fragments:
the child; the century's children;

the ones we do not know yet,
because they were flesh—

their secret, lilted home-
voices, faces caught
in lightning.   Found there

earth's bone-shadowed eyes;
her still life
your awkward printing:

starvation: light
moving down and up through light . . .

A ladder of stuff: a soft, gray,
broken oar, a feather,
a shoe, a child's pencil case;

light drawing us
to light,
day speaking to day . . .

Now, at dusk,
the man digging
saw himself approaching:

his half-smile looked past us: past himself:

the man chipping, at dusk,
under the trains, digging up
the dark, prosperous bluestone.

Silences: A Dream of Governments

From your eyes I thought
we could almost move   almost speak
But the way your face
held there, in the yellow air,
And that hand, writing down our names—
And the way the sun
shone right through us
Done with us

            Then
the plain astonishment— the air
broken open: just ourselves
sitting, talking; like always;
the kitchen window
propped open by the same
blue-gray dictionary.
August. Rain. A Tuesday.

Then, absence. The open room
suspended   The long street
gone off   quiet, dark.
The ocean floor. Slow
shapes glide by

Then, day
keeps beginning again: the same
stubborn pulse against the throat,
the same
listening for a human voice—
your name, my name

After Elegies (3)

August 12th
North Haven—

Here in the close, most clear sun,
on this worn wood porch, halfway
over the beating harbor,
under the round sky— the daylight moon's
luminous, fragile skull—

Halfway between sleep and waking,
I think of you,
my old brother,
difficult friend; and your moving on
from us to the dead
seems a few blocks' walk;
seems nothing.

Are you nothing   Nowhere we can find you

—But you look up
from your spread-out books and papers, you say
—But now I can't hear what you're saying,
and how can you hear us now?

or see our rowing progress here? our bare arms
pulled—
       Earth pulled
to where it would not go.

The Messenger

I / The Father

In the strange house
in the strange town
going barefoot past the parents' empty room
I hear the horses   the fire   the wheel   bone wings
your voice.

I make my corners:
this table
this letter
this walk.

2

The night you died
by the time I got there to the Peter Bent Brigham Hospital
the guard said, It's no use your going up.
That was the first time you spoke to me dead—
from the high corner of the lobby.

The next night a friend said, Well these deaths
bring our own deaths, close.

3

But now, this is your voice
younger than mine; leaning over— say goodbye—
the fake gold Navy officer's sword
the square real gun.

4

Every night the freight train crossed the grown-over road
at the foot of the Neilsens' field, trailing its rusty
whistle. The fire, the wheel; fireflies.
The wall of stars. Real horses. I could go
anywhere. I could go to where you are.
I lie under the bank, my face on the wall of wet grass.
I can't go anywhere, No such thing my dear.

My mother has flour on her hands,
on her cheekbone. My father smiles his one smile
gray and white on the wall. She pushes
her hair back from her eyes. His eyes
settle. On us.

II / The Messenger

You are the messenger
my half-brother, I have seen you before,
you have visited me before,
in the hallways of a school, a hospital,
in a narrow hotel room once,
once on a dirt road in August.

2

I lean on the oak grain of this desk,
the grain of your body, your hair,
your long back. This plum
is darker than your mouth
I drink its salty sweetness   its leaf-smell
from your tongue. Sleep;
your dark head at my breasts

                            Turns

to a boy's head, you are Allan   my brother
Johnny DeSoto, nine
Philip   my brother
David

Your hand is my father's sure, square hand,
it is not too late, digging down through the sand
to show me the water

You turn, say something in your sleep

You are my sister   I hold you warm in my hand   her breast
You trace my breasts

3
My eyes were clenched, they are opening . . .
everything, nothing . . .
We aren't afraid.
The earth drips through us

Now I want to live forever
Now I could scatter my body easily
if it was any use

now that the earth
has rained through us
green   white
green green grass.

4
You say you came to say if I live without you
I'll live. That's always been your story.

III / The Hill

The dogwood blossoms stand in still, horizontal planes
at the window. In mist. Small gray figures
climb away up the green hill. Carrying precision tools wrapped in
      oilcloth.
Some push their bicycles. —Wait, I'm coming, no this time I mean
      it

now I could scatter my body
if it was any use

saying again
if you do not teach me I shall not learn

—First, you see, you must be still. Touch nothing.
Here, in this room. To look at nothing, to listen to nothing.
A long time. First, you see, you must open your clenched hands.
You must carry your mother and your father at your breasts.

I stand on all fours, my fur
is warm; warm organs, the male and the female.
The earth is light and warm around us.
We lick our cracked old worries
like blood away from our faces, our haunches, we
nudge each other, all our white fur, goodbye, goodbye . . .

saying again there is a last
even of last times

I wake up with one hand holding hard to the other hand.
My head rests on oilcloth. A quiet voice laughs, and says again,

—You were going to go without me?
That was always your story.

Two Translations

Huub Oosterhuis:
Orpheus

Orpheus like a farmer
behind his plow of flutes
found in a dream the wound   the damp
place where the earth
quivers like a windpipe
and went down there.

Having been driven through woods
turned to rock   shifted by ice
fingers worn out with sailing
he got past the dog
and saw they were all dead there
except Eurydice.

Who lived in a barrel of zinc
brightly lit up
and had her love's doorframe
staves of a bed   a tree
swelling about her own underleaf white
sloping body
waiting for him but almost
unknowingly.

Enlisted with god he served seven years
shepherd   doorman   or he threaded wires
that would blow up thresholds   sink boats
direct the sun
and, to claim her, he became
wisely poorer.

Sometimes thought I'll walk into the countryside
like a horse
won't eat   will drown
it's better so
But did not want to and knew why not
the next day and the following he did his work
and waited.

After another seven years she could come along
it was as if he felt the worn spots
all over her
she had grown aimless
fat from sitting and sleeping
Could it be the snake   the thirst
he thought, when I play the flute
she may follow   she may

once again turn beautiful
as she used to be.

All right then she follows him
and why shouldn't she
she is nobody else and his tall back
is older is more hairy
but still the one she always
used to caress.

Then suddenly he no longer knew
whether it was she
the tune having escaped him
The forest as in every underworld
was doing well he saw
what had decayed was resurrected
He did not look back.

Sleeping they go on without a sound
She dreams   You and I were walking
I'm waking up
the skins over my eyes are still black
from waiting for your eyes   Look at me

———
35

if you love me she calls
Run still faster

Running on stripped nerves   I have
not looked around he calls and we shall
dearest see the earth
until our second death.
Over the water
sunlight blows before the wind
the grass is dark   creatures pass by
He walks and no longer knows
whether or not he did look back
and where the earth is
underneath   above

Osip Mandelstam:
394

Toward the empty earth
falling, one step faltering—
some sweetness, in this
unwilling hesitance—

she walks, keeping
just ahead of her friends,
the quick-footed girl,
the boy, one year younger.

A shy freedom draws her, her hobbled step
frees her, fires her, and it seems
the shining riddle in her walk
wants to hold her back:

the riddle, that this spring weather
is for us the first mother:
the mother of the grave.
And this will keep beginning forever.

There are women,
the damp earth's flesh and blood:

every step they take, a cry,
a deep steel drum.

It is their calling
to accompany those who have died;
and to be there, the first
to greet the resurrected.

To ask for their tenderness
would be a trespass against them;
but to go off, away from them—
no one has the strength.

Today an angel; tomorrow
worms, and the grave;
and the days after
only lines in chalk.

The step you took
no longer there to take.

Flowers are deathless. Heaven is round.
And everything to be is only talk.

—*Voronezh. 4 May 1937*

Solitudes

Some of the signs suggest that you feel a leaf or other part of a plant. A string leads from the top of the sign to the plant.

—Braille sign on the Miwok Trail, Muir Woods

The bird a nest, the spider a web, man friendship.

—Blake

December 21st

How will I think of you
"God-with-us"
a name: a word

and trees paths stars this earth
how will I think of them

and the dead I love   and all absent friends
here-with-me

and table: hand: white coffee mug:
a northern still life:

and you
without a body

quietness

and the infant's red-brown mouth   a star
at the star of a girl's nipple . . .

Sanctuary

People pray to each other. The way I say "you" to someone else,
respectfully, intimately, desperately. The way someone says
"you" to me, hopefully, expectantly, intensely . . .
—Huub Oosterhuis

.

You   who I don't know   I don't know how to talk to you

—What is it like for you there?

Here . . . well, wanting solitude; and talk; friendship—
The uses of solitude. To imagine; to hear.
Learning braille. To imagine other solitudes.
But they will not be mine;
to wait, in the quiet; not to scatter the voices—

What are you afraid of?

What will happen. All this leaving. And meetings, yes. But death.
What happens when you die?

". . . not scatter the voices,"

Drown out. Not make a house, out of my own words. To be quiet in
another throat; other eyes; listen for what it is like there. What
word. What silence. Allowing. Uncertain: to drift, in the
restlessness . . . Repose. To run like water—

42

What is it like there, right now?

Listen: the crowding of the street; the room. Everyone hunches in against the crowding; holding their breath: against dread.

What do you dread?

What happens when you die?

What do you dread, in this room, now?

Not listening. Now. Not watching. Safe inside my own skin.
To die, not having listened. Not having asked . . . To have scattered life.

Yes I know: the thread you have to keep finding, over again, to follow it back to life; I know. Impossible, sometimes.

What Happened

I don't know what happened, some very low time for my friend;
she said, —Come over; she couldn't talk, but come over anyhow.

My friend, have I ever befriended you? Helper and friend, will you
be befriended?

You talked along, quickly, forceably, about this thing and that, as
you do; you handed me coffee; I felt as if we were traveling at
some speed; in a taxi; I was looking at you through glass, you
looked back at me now and then, for a minute, through the glass;
so much grief in your eyes. Almost disinterested—

I asked, —What happened? Then, in your rush of talk, you told
me stories, about old friends, people you met, you showed me books,
photographs I'd like, you fed me, you entertained me.

Am I the unknowable one? Does my listening make just a white
place, like the space a person who is growing blind sees growing on
the page?

Suddenly you stopped walking around the room, stopped smiling.
You sat down, across from me; you said,
    —You and I are the same, in terrible ways.

Then furiously, talking very fast, you told me about my life:
How I go on repeating, over and over, my stupid leap for
home, where there's nothing; a homeless world; what else
did I think I was doing with X, last year; what good did
I think work could do; or anything else; knowing now how
things are: what would I do?

Telling me about your life:
It's always like that: you leap, you think for a minute you
have found something; Nothing; Terrible; there are only
distractions, crowding around over the surface of things.
—Now what would I do. People don't kill themselves, just
because they know how things are, know the world is
like this; they aren't so rational.
Asking yourself:
—What would you do—

To wait. To imagine . . . I just sat there, blind; not-there;
my friend, and I, not seeing each other; seeing instead some mask
or sign; consenting to be some mask or sign.
The half-cured man in Mark's gospel, who answers Christ, "I can
see men as if they were trees, but walking."
To not see, not be seen: the sudden fear: like a déjà vu: is there

45

anyone I do see? anyone I know? even of the closest ones. Or who knows me?

To listen for what it is like there. To wait . . . Contagion: our grief and fury ran down like electricity into the ground, leaving the room a fiction, an empty space. The glass didn't shift, we couldn't touch only ghosts: the unreachable teller, the unreachable listener; both going silent, unbefriended.

—But there are shelters; they break down, but they mend; we can live, that way. But I didn't say anything; you were telling me another story, smiling your strong smile, showing me more things: I couldn't get past them; there wasn't time.

I keep talking to you, here, in my head; but I don't know what to say: not enough:

Yet the cell is only the rudiment. A human being is made up of about 1,000 billion cells, a drop of blood containing 5 million of them . . .

To wait. To imagine. Learning braille.

———

Once I was talking to a friend, a religious man, about the closeness
of friendships in childhood, and he said, What you're talking
about, is God. Mercy on our gropings, our silences. Our harm.
Mercy, or nothing is enough; mercy on our deceptions, endless, our
endless longings; our words that go like smoke into smoke. Some
shelter,
for my friend,
for each one, quiet, talking,
alone, together, to trust, to rest in a while.

Turn (2): After Years

January. At the window
wet-dark twigs and branches of young birch
reach up, cross each other:
a road map, a map of rivers . . .

Hundreds of drops of the freezing rain
hold the day's gray light close:
silver   hundreds of stars

I think of you
looking out your city window— everyone away
—a thin, light-eyed, noticing child,
standing so quiet

—a tall man, restless, faithful, your light eyes always
not-here, always here . . .

I think of our lives
different   the same

the years, half-blown,

What we had, we have.

Now I can turn,
—now, without want, or harm—
turn back to the room, say your name:
say: *other*   say, *thou* . . .

The Burden of Memory

New Hampshire
January 28th

Do you remember, last time we saw each other, how the first thing
you said was, "Isn't it good we're always friends?" And then, both
of us, I think, feeling stopped, empty-handed; past the high,
brittle day of meeting like lovers, five years ago; just ourselves
again, groping for friendship again. And then, you talked so
easily, like when we were kids; more than you ever have, to me,
about your life, now; yourself.

And I remembered, what I'd known before— I wonder if it's so, for
you, too— being drawn, with you, by memory, back to a life that
seems less harmful . . . "student days" . . . —And what good was
that? That memory itself drawing us to harm.   But then,
ourselves again; some mercy; taking in that angry sorrow, part of
us, a healed bone that does go on hurting; a mark of mercy; and
we could be quiet again, and talk.

And then, here in this solitude, this quiet, remembering so many
things I'd forgotten, I was thinking back to those days: you, an
"older man," going with L.; I suppose you were both seventeen . . .
Do you remember, one day when we were talking, I forget what
about, but my saying, "You're such a friend to me," and you said,

"Yes and I always will be." And then I could tell you about that time, in California. —I want to talk to you now about it, again; I've never talked to anyone else about it, and it's been alive with me here again— do you remember it? I don't think you could; the whole family, over at another Navy family's place, for a picnic. 1943— I was nine. I was off from the other kids when I saw it. In a shed, or garage, I don't remember: a wooden building, pretty far off from the house. There was a barrel, but I could see into it, and there were heads in there, people's heads, cut in half. In something like formaldehyde maybe, they were kept so life-like. I never knew why I didn't run for one of the other kids, to look. —I could only finally tell, on the way home; I got sick again, in the car, and I told them. Of course my parents said Nonsense, it was impossible; but very angry. A little later they said I must be very overtired, and after that they were always very careful that I should get plenty of sleep. —I could never tell anyone again. It was so real: but it *was* impossible, it couldn't have been there. I must be crazy. And what a creepy kind of crazy. What becomes of people like that? —And some awful shame, worse than any shame I've ever felt.

And then I could tell you, that day, ask you, if you thought I was crazy; tell you about the shame. And you said, "I think it happened. In some way. I don't know. It doesn't matter, what way."

———

—You mean a dream or something. I *know* it wasn't a dream. But I know, it couldn't—

—We were around the same age. I saw things . . . we heard about things.

—But you were there, in the war.

—It doesn't matter. I don't know. It was 1943. People knew things. We do; we know things now. And here we are, alive. Fine; playing, in peace. No wonder for the shame. What will we do? I don't know . . . But it doesn't mean we did those things. *You* know that.

I wonder if you had any idea, how saving that was, what you said.

The same lightening of things, talking to you now, in this room—

And you— I wonder, have I been companionable to you, too, been there, any use, in your silences, your aloneness— your letter the other day, saying, "a low time"— I wish I could touch your hand, there, now . . .

———

—*We do know things*. That memory, back with me now, and the
shame. Now. *What will we do*

*How long can we stay interested in the lone man's liberty? . . .
I'm afraid [the individual], being saved by himself, will be lost
by himself . . .* —Montale

February 9th

The consolation of another solitude, miles away, years away; in
the next room; its words, its silences;
waiting to be listened for; imagined.
Kinship.   Meetings.

We all line up to ask each other for help.
Millions.
One.

>   *Line up*— in Swedish— associations of people lining up
>   for food, shelter . . . —Tranströmer

My whole life, I've never been hungry. Or without a room; with
warmth, and light. Warm; fed. At the edges of this world. People
who *are driven out of their minds by good living.* —Milosz

Aloneness: physical feelings: cold, hunger.   Wrongfulness.
Solitude— choosing to hope to live— holding close in the cold

Emily Dickinson: . . . *test's severe repairs are permitted all.*
>   *. . . It is difficult not to be fictitious in so fair a*
>   *place, but test's severe repairs are permitted all.*

Not to be fictitious.
I can't think of the first word.

Uncovering; unthickening. Changes
. . . the memories I can't look out past, to look around: this room—

Look: they join you to every fragility   here

Your letter, from August: *At the same time*
there is such a strong sense, of uncovering
and naming to the point of losing what you
may have had . . . It was like touching the
center and therefore losing it, emptying it
of what you might have been able to hold on to.

        And your letter, saying, *No one has*
        ever asked me about "everyday life" . . .
        Raising your son, teaching, in Maine,
        alone painting, paintings not seen
        changing   your memories changing
        We must account for our existence
        and it helps to talk openly if at all
        possible. I will try,

And your letter, saying, *We are*
indeed graced by our mutual friendship

with B_____. She has saved my life more
than once and most especially this fall.
No doubt you have heard from her about

And you, writing, this letter today,
the hidden way of each of us, buried

kinship
a buried crystal holding the sun

kinship
the salt of our hands
touching

changing

memories changing

Higginson: *. . . I have the greatest desire to see you, always feeling*
that perhaps if I could once take you by the hand I
might be something to you;

Dickinson: *You were not aware that you saved my Life.*

———

"Love and Work":
Freud Dying

He could watch his soul, a line drawing, almost a cartoon, rise up,
out of his mouth, past the footpaths up a steep, concentric
mountain, to enter another city: a vast, black and white city,
at the top of space, precisely edged in blue and red and gold leaf.
September. A gray, light absence of God.

All his books were there, in his room; and the rugs over the sofas,
and the small Egyptian statues, the Greek heads. Men and women
with sad, lively eyes came and asked to study with him. Friends
and colleagues were there, "both of the past & of the present."

But the first hour, resting for a minute, from his walk, on a bench
in a green square near his house, he fell asleep. He dreamed he
was walking, deep in the ocean; he was both male and female.
The dome of the world fitted perfectly over the ocean floor. The
slow currents filled his mind with a reasoning peacefulness he
thought he must remember. High clouds of sunlight moved through
the water.

No one here was marked off, by coloring or sex or money. Still, as
they walked slowly by him, their faces held some questioning,
calm sorrow. The dream was like a voice, the singsong rhythms of
a voice he had known a long time, but without words, an old
story. He wondered if someone had told it to him.

57

He woke up: he wanted to touch someone; to listen, again, to the consolation of that voice. Familiar voices waited around him in his room. One spoke his name, a strange sounding word, now. Most he wanted, to go back to his dream, where there were no Jews, and no fame of accomplishment to save them.

No, it must just be that he didn't know anything yet, about that strange, slow place, its darknesses; he had to go back and listen; walk there, and think:

—*London, September 1939*

Letter from a Stranger

You said, you know what I mean: one winter, you looked and saw
a river branching in the black sycamore branches, silver
veins of roads rising and ending in icy twigs at your window;
an awful time. Then spring came and you said
you *learned to love Lincoln again*; the first leaves came
and you saw Lincoln's *kind, grave face, drawn there*
in the leaves, in the light.
How can I answer your letter? words from your life
bring me home to my life. So safe
now, that I can leave it again, now
the milky quiet. The warm straw.

"*Actuarial File*"

Orange peels, burned letters, the car lights shining on the grass,
everything goes somewhere— and everything we do— nothing
ever disappears. But changes. The roar of the sun in photographs.
Inching shorelines. Ice lines. The cells of our skin; our meetings,
our solitudes. Our eyes.

A bee careens at the window here; flies out, released: a life
without harm, without shame.   That woman, my friend,
circling against her life, a married life; that man, my friend,
solitary, anarchic, driving away from home; them driving, to each
other—

I know, the hard, half-lost, knowing will; the cold first loneliness
again, outside the commonweal, unmoving;

But to say, *I know*— is there any touch in it?

> The words in my dream: "actuarial file." *Actuary, 1. A
> registrar or notary, who keeps records of the acts of a
> court* . . .

To be there; to listen; not invade. Another solitude . . .

————

60

I watch her face. The lines of will, kindness, hunger. Silence. She moves from one thing to another thing in the kitchen, looks out the window at the other apartment windows . . . A woman moves around, across the courtyard, making supper. How many people is she making supper for? Now the woman waters the plants. What is she thinking about. Her head, her arm, look peaceful . . .

"Everything that happens, happens once and for all. Is this true? If so, what then?"

Yes. Your story; all of your hope; what you do, breaks. Changes. "If so, what then?" Nothing disappears. And you do last;

The words in the open page of her notebook, *I'm so cold. My head hurts.*

Come stay here, at my place, a while. —Someday we will be able to say, I did this thing; I did that other thing; I was that woman. Someday, we will be able to take it in, that violence, hold it in our hands . . . And the ones who come after us, maybe they can understand us; forgive us; as we do forgive our parents, our

———

grandparents, moving so distantly through their lives . . . their
silences . . .
And the ones we were with   maybe our friendship can change,
can mend . . .

Come stay here. Things change . . .

She stays home;

Not to invade   Wait, here, in the quiet

Lines from a Story

*I remembered . . . [my grandfather] said that if you let your blood
run, you make yourself better. If there are spirits in you that
want to go, they will leave with the blood.*
—An Eskimo woman, to Robert Coles

Mother   your quiet face
already at eight years old a survivor's face:

You say   there is no mother or father,
say, fear,   It is too cold
here, you say, I am alive,   I will
hold myself in my own hands.

The white beach in that photograph, white
lake, white sky, a page . . .   your story
that I know in such spent outlines . . .

But still your hands
hold me to you, here,
your voice reads to me, still,
—your voice that forgot itself
in other people's words—

You never thought you knew things.

And I have begun, so late, to trust what I love!
To hope
to gather in the rest.
Or let it go:
I cut my arm, it bled;
a long dawn
opening to here:

in my own hands
in the quiet   listening
—I send this page to you,
from memory:
lines from a story, about two friends
who lived in distant towns:
"—If I could talk to you now,
I believe we could be so simple,
if you could talk to me,
then we could be so still."

March 21st

Out of 92 natural elements, we could never have predicted man. We could never even get to the wetness of water, the miracle of ordinary water. Water is one of the strangest substances in all of chemistry.
—George Wald

5 a.m.

Waking. Something, dry, without shape, moving toward the tilted faces, the voices, of the dream,

The room the clearing in the trees moving

Now, the thumbed line of daylight, behind them,
finding the room,   its lines, down, across—
my body   finding again   "I"

The words from a dream of yours, twenty years ago,
"Relay locality"

And you, my father, my brother, your face in my dream, receding,
your voice saying, what they told me you did say,
—*They're getting farther away; but it isn't them, it's me; I'm
getting old;* /

Your voice, leaving: and still the day

And you, my brother,
—*No wonder for the shame.*

And you, my mother, my sister,
our talk   our stillness   now

And you, my father, my mother,
"unlosable friend"

saying again
—*Here is the life outside the window,*
  here is the earth, the water, here is
  fire, the blood, the breath moving through your own hands:

  your work   everyone you love

And you, my sister, writing,
the hidden way of each of us, buried